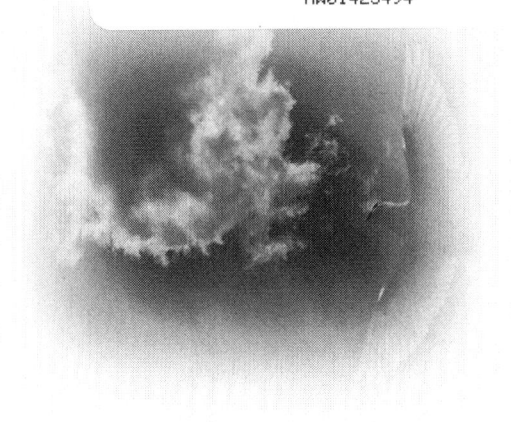

Lost in The Storm...
Found in the Rainbow

...to all who keep on turning back
it happens just don't stay
there's healing in the rainbow
and Jesus is the way

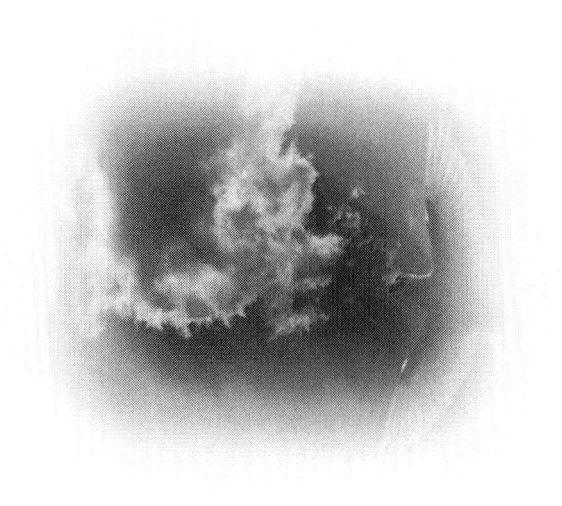

Lost in The Storm...
Found in the Rainbow

"I have placed my rainbow in the clouds. It is the sign of my covenant with you and with all the earth." Genesis 9:13 (NIV)

Poetry and Prose to Re-ignite the Spirit
By P. H. Mathis

...to all who keep on turning back
it happens just don't stay
there's healing in the rainbow
and Jesus is the way

This book contains poetic expressions, thoughts and scriptures that affirm why life has stormy seasons and the *Shelter* found in the rainbow…

His name is Jesus and He's waiting to cover you!

Scriptures taken from THE HOLY BIBLE, NEW INTERNATIONAL VERSION®, NIV® Copyright © 1973, 1978, 1984, 2011 by Biblica, Inc.® Used by permission. All rights reserved worldwide.

This book should not be reproduced in any form without permission from the publisher. Exceptions are made in the case of quotations used in religious related publications, articles or reviews.

Printed in the United States of America

Unlock Publishing House, Inc.

Copyright © 2016

P. H. Mathis

ISBN 978-0-9967941-2-1

Contents

Forward

Introduction

Chapter 1
Discover *JESUS*

No Sin Again
Finding Familiar Ground
Pray For Them
What Jesus Did
Who Owns the Fence
Naked Now Free

Chapter 2
Submit *to JESUS*

Change
I've Done This and That…Now I Do Jesus
A Clearer View
When I Wake
The O Word
Hallelujah! You'll be Set Free

Chapter 3
Receive *JESUS*

Receive
Jesus, the Inherited Legacy
Where Do I Go From Here
Increase
The Flavor of His Favor
Be Still

Chapter 4
Walk *with JESUS*

What Happens When We Walk With You
A Turn of Events
Favor
Move Over
When In Life's Valley Season…
Don't Miss the Boat
The Purpose For Which We Exist
Shelter from the Storm

Thank you…

Forward

This book contains poetry and prose inspired by discovering how lost I was while listening and acting out life based on the influence of the enemy (Satan). One day I found I had another choice, I had a Savior named Jesus and now I live under His influence.

My Jesus is your Jesus, so let His redeeming powers shelter and save you from life's storms.

Lost Now Found

Didn't know that I was lost
Never took the time to see
The things that I was doing
Would be the death of me

But one day out of the blue
My actions sat me down
I heard my spirit speaking
The place where Gods now found

My life did pass before me
The ugly I had to see
I cried so much on that day
Didn't believe what I had come to be

The revelation before me
Of things I did for years
I finally realized was not the way
God intended for me to live

So I thank Him for that day
The day when all hell broke loose
The day when Jesus was increased
and I myself reduced

For he has rescued us
from the dominion of darkness
and brought us into the kingdom
of the Son he loved. Colossians 1:13

Introduction

How often have you looked back on your life and had regrets? When I think about my life, I'm often reminded of the little voice I heard telling me something I shouldn't do but like many, I did it anyway. Many of the regrets I have are because I insisted on doing things my way but if I had done it differently, I would not have the material to write this book. I would not be able to share the valuable lessons I learned of which the most important; the voice I always ignored, was the one I should have listened to.

As life's journey continues, I understand why people follow wrong voices and make bad choices. I understand better why I turned the wheel of "free will" to the far left instead of just driving down the narrow highway. The safe road, the one the Bible says is less traveled. I also understand that if we never realize we need saving, we would never realize we need a Savior! Nonetheless, as life offers regrets and we miss answering the right voice, God never gives up on us and He knows just where to find us when we are ready!

On August 5th of 2010 I discovered how lost I was while listening to the wrong voice for much of my life. I also learned the meaning of a message I had heard that same year at a Women's Retreat; the speaker explained, "You can determine the magnitude of your latent talents by the multitude of enemies camped around you." I also learned on August 5th that we don't have to come to a near death experience to receive from God.

Today I know that God's mercy is greater than any mess we could conjure up. I now walk a straight path, standing firm and believing the things I've read in the Bible. I embrace the narrow road, the one less traveled, *"for wide is the gate and broad is the road that leads to destruction..."* I also thank God daily for the ones who watched over me and held me as I stumbled because now I can help and hold up another who may be lost in the storm.

On the day when my hell broke loose I realized that Jesus was always there waiting for me to *Discover Him, Submit to Him, Receive from Him and Walk with Him.* So…

> For all who keep on turning back
> It happens just don't stay
> there's healing in the rainbow
> and Jesus is the way!"

Those along the path are the ones who hear, and then the devil comes and takes away the word from their hearts, so that They may not believe and be saved. Luke 8:12, 14-15

Lost in The Storm...
Found in the Rainbow

...didn't know that I was lost
never took the time to see
the things that I was doing
would be the death of me

so I thank God for that day
the day all hell broke loose
the day when Jesus was increased
and I myself reduced...

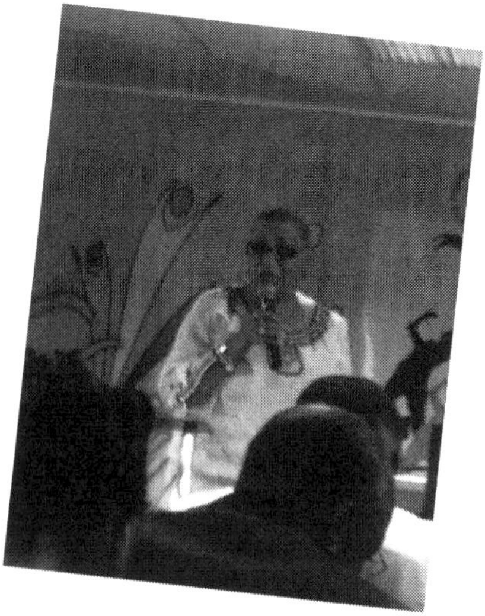
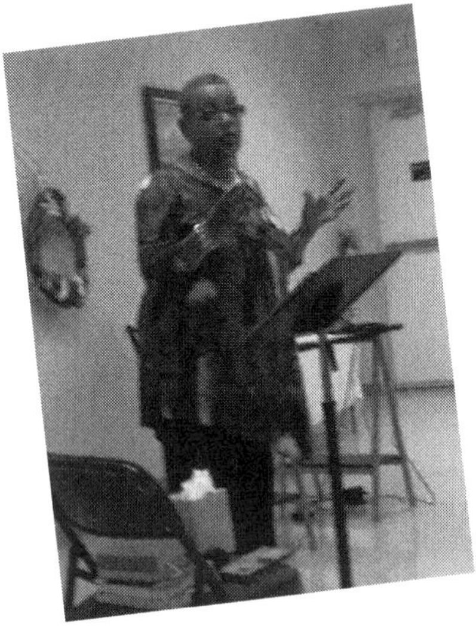
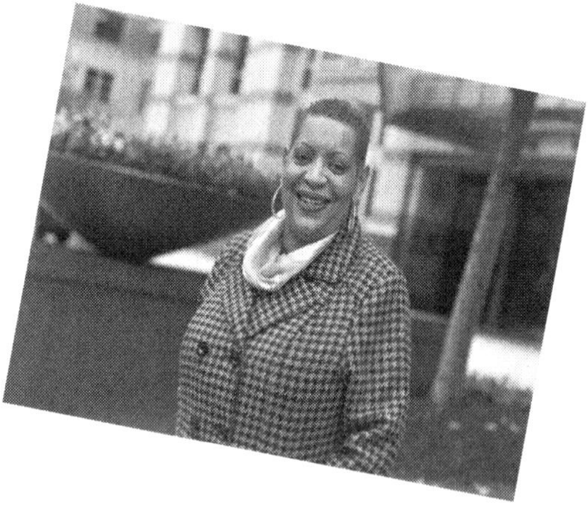

Have you flipped through the pages of your life lately and found any regrets? When I did stop long enough to honestly look at my past and my present, it was on a day the bottom dropped from underneath my feet. The very foundation of my existence had disintegrated and that was the day when, "All hell broke loose!" The day my life passed before me, the day when the paradigm shift of wrong living showed up and I could do nothing more than cry out, "God I can't do this anymore, please help me!"

On that life altering day, my marriage of 22+ years would combust right before my eyes and along with it, I had to contend with a flood of very vivid reminders of all the bad decisions I had made. The many years of taking chance after chance with my life and the lives of those I loved. Making decisions of detriment while co-existing in a shell with a smooth exterior but a crumbled mess on the inside – twas my life.

The cause and effect of my detriment; the very source of wrong decision making appeared to stem from the two distinct voices one hears through life; the one saying, "No don't do that" and the other saying "yes, do it!" You know the image of the devil and angel portrayed in cartoons sitting on someone's shoulder. Well, like Eve, the voice that said "Eat it" is the same voice I listened to for years.

The voice of the "enemy of this world", the devil, who clearly meant what he said in John 10:10, *"I came to kill, steal and destroy"*, was the source of my wrong decision making; my spiritual death and the death (physical and spiritual) of those built like me. The ones who still struggle with bondage, not knowing they are valuable pieces in the treasure chest of our Lord – no matter the brokenness.

Listening to that wrong voice, making wrong decisions and experiencing a day when the bottom of my life dropped out, allowed me to; **discover** *Jesus*, **submit** *to Jesus*, **receive** *Jesus* and **walk** *with Jesus*, who is the other voice in John 10:10 that said, "*...But I came so that they would have life and have it to the full.*"

My wrong decisions were a part of the means to <u>my</u> end *(...but whoever loses his life for my sake and the Gospel's will save it Mark 8:5).* The decisions I made then, are now my witness to the presence behind the voice I always ignored, the voice of the Holy Spirit.

The lessons from my wrong decisions are now the foundation on which I stand to minister to those God has assigned to me, the ones that I will share who Jesus is and why. I walk a straight path now and I thank God for keeping me as I stumbled. He has lead me to Christ, "T*he solid rock on which I stand*"!

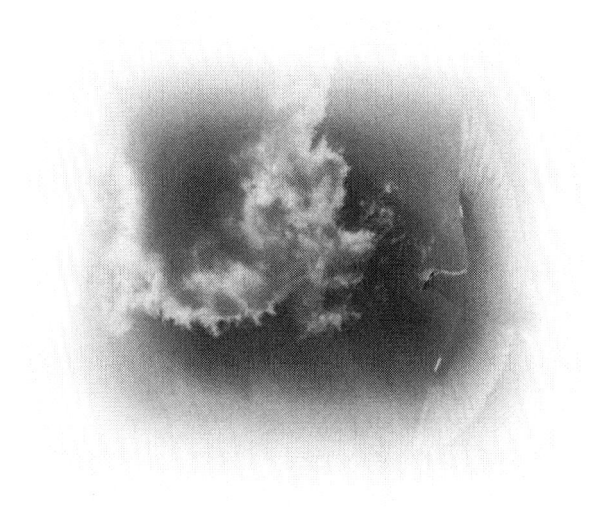

Chapter 1

Discover JESUS

…and the sin power that has ruled your life
is now broken!

Discover

I believe mirrors in opposition to sleep because in order to discover anything, you really need to be awake. For many years I was in a deep sleep, a comatose state inflicted by the fairy dust of deception, sprinkled in my eyes by Satan. This sleep prevented me from moving into and through the areas of my life that God had created doors for me to open. Once through those doors, I would have discovered my purpose. However, sleep came upon me because many times I allowed the thief to "seek me out…steal, kill and destroy" all of what God had planned for me. My eyes were blinded by the fairy dust, each time I tried to achieve something God had planned for me to do.

In the first chapter, "Discover" I share that no matter how long you are asleep, when you awake, Jesus is waiting to partner with you. He is ready to wipe your eyes and open the door. He is willing to be your forever escort, seeing you through and holding your hand as you take on life, just by merely saying, "Jesus, I need you".

My prayer is that the very simple words offered in the first chapter will open up a place in your heart that will ignite a fire in your spirit. This fire will arouse a curiosity in you, then you will want to know exactly what God had in mind, when He created you – because <u>He did have a plan</u> (see Jeremiah 29:11)

Wake-up all who slumber and be free from the bondage of slavery and death handed down by the enemy. Discover the life offered to all who believe in Jesus - He is waiting for you!

> *"Our old sinful selves were crucified with Christ so that sin might lose its power in our lives. We are no longer slaves to sin. For when we died with Christ we were set free from the power of sin…" Romans 6:6 – 7:1*

No Sin Again

Never knew before I got here
Those before me paved the way
There was sin entrenched in the bloodline
So now I stop and pray

So easy when I lived in sin
Not knowing it was attached to me
I thank you God for scripture
Explaining generational iniquity

The knowledge through your Word dear Lord
Has shown me the way
How to clean the slate for those to come
So again I stop and pray

Yes I've done this and that and more
Didn't actually know why
Then Jesus came and rescued me
Now all I do is cry

Rejoicing through my many tears
For the path is now made clear
For the coming of my loved ones God
That you have held so near

Their road will be much smoother
Not needing to test the way
For the generational curse before us
Is finally prayed away

Finding Familiar Ground

Sometimes life is no stranger
to the things that keep you down
This mean ole world has lots of stuff
that somehow keeps you bound
The flesh will keep you tied up
not wanting you to heed
God's instructions written just for you
then Satan plants his seed

He finds all of your weaknesses
he starts when you're very young
He captures your mind unknowingly
so he becomes the one
The one that directs your every move
all decisions that you make
He fools you into believing
you are making no mistakes

His purpose is to keep you
from the treasure God has for you
He stays in every thought you have
in all you say and do
But ultimately the decision is yours
to take the other course
And find through God that he's the one
that he's the other source

The source that has provided
the instruction on how to succeed
But leaves it up to us to acquire
a thirst to want to read

For in God's Word we will discover
that the road was not that rough
For the ground is much much smoother
once you purge the fleshy stuff

Pray For Them

The enemy wears many faces
He hides in the hearts of men
The place where love was planted
The place where God has been
He takes the nicest people
The ones with friendly smiles
They fill the pews on Sundays
They walk the center aisle

The devil knows just where to go
The church is his favorite place
He knows that Jesus will return
And he must win the race
To capture all the souls he can
That is his devious plot
He smiles with great excitement
As he claims the one's he's got

The ones that choose the here and now
Forsaking the after life
That life which God has promised
Where there's no more pain and strife

So if you have decided
To hang out where the light is dim
For the ones who have chosen Jesus
Let's hurry and pray for them

What Jesus Did

He tore and turned me
Sift and stirred me
Placed and pushed me on

He picked and pruned me
Focused and fertilized me
Straightened and stood me up

He caught and cleaned me
Loved and lifted me
Attached and assigned me others

His promise He kept
So I accept
My assignment
To bring Him another

Who Owns the Fence?

There is this fence where some are perched
not knowing who's the owner
As with most fences there are two sides
on one you'll be a loner
The folks that choose to slide and glide
from one side to the other
Forsake all that is theirs in Christ
as ransomed sisters and brothers

Then what is sad about some folks
who know who God is
They also know the devil
but forgot all that he did
And why he fell from heaven
and landed on the earth
The place he stopped to build his fence
The place where some still perch
They think they have a choice
so day to day they take
A chance with their salvation
which is a HUGE mistake

There are two sides to this fence
then there's the fence itself
There's also a lifeline straight from God
that he did send to help
God doesn't want us to ever fall
or even sit up on the fence
So He sent a lifeline found in Christ
to use as our defense
So if you need to ponder this
And can't make the right decision
Perched on the fence that Satan owns

will cause you much division
You'll separate from God
and what He offers you
If you decide to take the fence
the devil and his crew

Naked Now Free

Stripped away with nothing to wear
The chill did feel like death
But praise I give for nakedness
Cause the cold did clean my mess
There is no real importance
When peace you cannot find
All twisted in the things of life
We need to leave behind
The stripping was your process Lord
To purge each part of me
And now I'm witness to those chained
Who cry to be set free

will cause you much division
You'll separate from God
and what He offers you
If you decide to take the fence
the devil and his crew

Naked Now Free

Stripped away with nothing to wear
The chill did feel like death
But praise I give for nakedness
Cause the cold did clean my mess
There is no real importance
When peace you cannot find
All twisted in the things of life
We need to leave behind
The stripping was your process Lord
To purge each part of me
And now I'm witness to those chained
Who cry to be set free

Chapter 2

Submit to JESUS

…and the sin power that has ruled your life is now broken!

*S*ubmit is an action not always warmly embraced in today's world. Many would define it as a weakness. Another unspoken reality is that we live in a world that embraces many strengths as weaknesses and weaknesses as strengths. Perfect example, a man who would submit to his feelings and cry (actually shed tears) would be considered weak. There are many family's that teach their boys not to cry – especially in public. In actuality, when a man cries, it exhibits character strengths. It shows he is in touch with his human condition. Nonetheless, there is promise from God for those who are humble. *"Humble yourselves, therefore, under the mighty hand of God so that at the proper time he may exalt you," 1 Peter 5:6*

When pondering the word submit, I was moved to recall situations where people submit to things in life, not having a choice in the matter. As children we (should) submit to the authority of our parents, or hopefully a penalty ensued. As students in school, in order to get good grades you must submit to studying and if not, a penalty ensued. As adults we must submit to others in authority in order to be the benefactors of certain societal benefits and if we don't - we pay a penalty.

When I entered my pre-teen years, I often heard my mother reference my disobedience as me starting to smell myself. I didn't understand that phrase until I had my own children; just as I was a hard head they were too. Just as my mother laid down the penalty on me, I laid it down on them too. By the time I had my children, I had started to understand that disobedience without consequence destroys. What I love about "old school parenting" is you would eventually submit or the penalty phase would continue until you learned your lesson.

As an adult, unfortunately I did continue in disobedience in more areas than I care to think about especially as I started to remember the teachings of the Bible. I also suffered a greater penalty phase and that was time – something I could not recapture. Honestly, the same thing that was a deficit to my well-being as a child, plagued me as an adult. Listening to wrong voices and then making bad choices which caused many a heartache for me but God said in Joel 2:25, "I will give you back what you lost to the swarming locusts…" and God is a man that does not lie.

When I started submitting to the things of God, not only was there a reward, it inspired me to write the pieces in this next chapter. God has promised that if we believe and submit to Him and the authority of His Son, Jesus the Christ, "He will supply all of our needs…" So won't you submit yourselves to the promises of God, be free in the life offered in Jesus… he is waiting for you.

"Submit yourselves, then to God; Come near to God and he will come near to you." James 4:7-8 (NIV)

Change

What is it now that I should do
since all my world is filled with You
It was so easy when I lived in sin
and now that I begin again
The friends I thought I had are gone
And I know I did nothing wrong
I'm not complaining I'm blessed you see
so very in love with the brand new me
This change in me just had to be
so I could help some others see
We need to trust and have faith in You
cause You will cause a life break through
The turn-around is there for all
just go to God He'll stand you tall
This ain't no joke I swear to you
It is amazing what my God will do
When serious about the desire to change
then watch how God will re-arrange
He'll mold you into someone new
that's something you could never do
He'll remove the things that shouldn't be
He'll clean your slate and make you free
Don't be conflicted but convicted
do just what the Good Book says
It might seem hard when first you try
but please choose God instead
His favor He will cast on you
just watch what it will do
His amazing touch will make you see
just what it is that you should be
So take these words and know for sure
with God you will endure

His way is real I tell cause
no longer am I where I was
It wasn't me that did the fix
It was my God He's full of tricks!

I've done this and that but now I do Jesus

My life unwritten no map displayed
no course in which to take
Ashamed of much I did back then
all that I do forsake

I tripped and stumbled and fell a lot
really didn't listen at all
But Jesus came and picked me up
no longer do I fall

I'm following as an obedient child
just wanting always to please
Continuing on salvation's path
while staying on my knees

I pray each day for constant protection
I can't let my guard down
Cause the devil will slip in any crack
when he knows your heaven bound

He hates to lose - but me he has
no more do I welcome sin
I've done this and that but now I do Jesus
through him I know I'll win

A Clearer View

You let me see my future
Which sometimes was not so bright
I also heard your voice at times
While fast a sleep at night
I saw within my dreams
What appeared to be your face
It's something that I look for now
And need to keep this pace
I had to strip away the things
That always kept me stale
The things that seemed to always cause
Whatever I did to fail

So now that I can witness
How you help us down life's roads
Regrets oh yes I had a few
But now the stories told
No need to hide from truth
The blessings now are shared
No longer do I walk in fear
No longer am I scared

I'm not afraid to tell the many
About the habits I had
For they were really not my own
Just proof the devils bad
But I won't give him focus now
Because my view is clear
With 20/20 in my eyes
And God my chandelier

When I Wake

I woke because you shook me
What exactly did you want
If I appeared uninterested
Didn't mean to be nonchalant
I wasn't trying to ignore you
I guess you thought I was
Cause what you did to wake me up
Did cause more than a buzz
It started me to thinking
I couldn't get back to sleep
I started sifting through my life
A mound that was so steep
The truth in all the refuge
Was more than I could take
So back to sleep I go Dear Lord
I'll call you when I wake

The O Word

*O*ut of submission
it flows like running water

*O*bserving its importance
is what we have to do

*O*paque in its appearance
to those who don't believe

*O*mitting all its value
the blessing you won't receive

*O*bligated as a Believer
To embrace it everyday

*O*bstacles in life avoided
when there in it you stay

*O*ccupy it in your mind
and let it be your breath

*O*bject any interference
that would cause untimely death

*O*ffenses were forgiven
as He hung there on the cross

*O*ffering all that He could for us
so He did pay the cost

*O*vertook our sin and sickness
and death so we could live

*O*bedience is the O word
That thing that we must give

Hallelujah, You'll Be Set Free

When in doubt don't delay
Invoke God's power and there you stay
And never have another need
Another want another plea
Not ever caged again
Forgiven of all sin
Submit is all He ask
Your new life He'll unmask
No longer in bondage you'll be
Hallelujah you'll be set free
Not doubting who you are
God's bright and shining star
You'll light the way for others
And this is what you'll do
When once you have discovered
The things God has for you
You'll rejoice in who you'll be
Hallelujah, you've been set free!

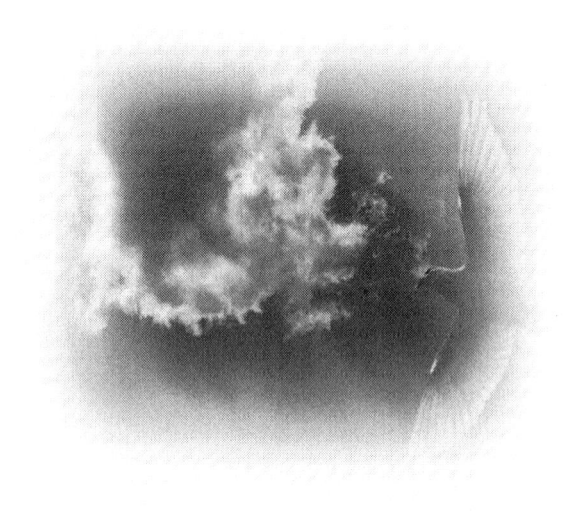

Chapter 3

Receive JESUS

…and the sin power that has ruled your life is now broken!

*R*eceive, was one of my favorite pass times as a child because it simply means – get! I loved to get as most children do. However, my mother would constantly remind me of the equal exchange required when one gets - one must also give. When I was very young, my mother would come home from work with some little surprise in her work bag for me. It could have been a slice of cake or a left over piece of her sandwich from lunch – it really didn't matter because it was for me, from my Mom and I was about to participate in my favorite pastime - getting something! I would be so excited when I heard her key turn the lock, I would say to myself "Yea, Mommy's home, wonder what she has for me." I knew she had brought me something in exchange for a smile, a hug, a kiss and the, "thank you Mommy", she always got from me.

As I better understand who God is, I know when we show kindness to each other and also let Him know that we are thankful for the things He does, He smiles and is happy. Hey, I can tell you, God has more gifts in His "workbag" than Mommy ever had! Actually, God is the biggest giver imaginable and doesn't require very much in return. However, He does want us to willingly submit and want from Him. The very big gifts God offers us are through His Son, Jesus and some of those gifts are; eternal life, salvation, hope, peace, life, light, love, forgiveness, freedom, healing and the best of all, Jesus himself! And all of that is ours just by simply saying, "Jesus, I want you in my life! – I give myself to you."

In life we will find roads with pot holes, detours, roundabouts, and various other diversions. I use to believe I had to literally fall in the mud and eat it before being convinced what it was. However, I was told by my mother, many times, "Mud is mud and you don't have to fall in it to know it – just listen to me!" Not only did Mama have goodies in her bag, she had goodies in her speech too.

Nonetheless, God wants so much for his children. He has provided instructions, restoration and provision, for everything we could imagine that will happen in our life time. God's love for us is so BIG and all He ask we do, is to RECEIVE His Son!

The Prayer of Salvation

"Father in Heaven I love you. I confess that I am a sinner. I believe that Jesus is your Son and that He died on a cross as payment for my sins. On the third day You raised Him from the dead, thank you for all you have done for me. Father, You are my very own Father now and I give my life to You, have Your way with me. I profess that Jesus Christ is Lord of my life and I will follow You forever. I pray this in Jesus name. Amen.

Receive

I say God I believe in you
Your Word does strengthen me
Each time I part the pages
I see the victory

So when life's troubles come
Remind me this one thing
The words I've read they live in me
With the power that they bring

The power that <u>did</u> heal me
The power from disease
The power from my brokenness
Your promise guarantees

In exchange for just one thing
That You have asked of me
That I would RECEIVE Your provision
And claim my victory

JESUS – The Inherited Legacy

There is no pretense in my stride
No exaggerated pride
No initials behind my name
Can't think of any fame
Just finally heard God speak
He said you've reached your peak
And now can receive your prize
The things He put aside
Just waiting for me to awake
My life I had to retake
No more thinking about the past
I'm now riding in first class
My mind's been altered anew
This is what Jesus will do
So I'll use the lessons I've learned
To help another turn
And find life is so good
Cause now it's understood
The other stuff was mess
To keep you from being blessed
With knowing what Jesus can offer you
When you finally push on through
And claim your destiny
Your inherited legacy

Where do I go from here?

Where do I go Dear Lord
With all you've given me
How do I step into the things
I never knew could be

Now that the door is open
And my eyes they see brand new
Increase in me the courage needed
To continue to step on through

Walking boldly in these new clothes I wear
Knowing approval from others I don't need
But continued guidance from you dear Lord
And increase in spiritual maturity

As I continue in this direction
The path you put me on
Oh won't you place in front of me
The angels who'll keep me strong
So I can help somebody else
There are many out there like me
The ones who've yet to meet my Jesus
And know He is the key

So as I start I finish
Knowing that Your ear is near
Oh won't you whisper to me Lord
Where do I go from here?

Increase

The more I flex
The more He favors
The more I submit
The more He supplies
The more I believe
The more He bestows
The more I accept
The more He anoints
The more I cry
The more He cleanses
The more I diminish me
The more I'm increased in Him

The Flavor of His Favor

The flavor of His favor
is good to the taste
Replaces all the other stuff
that keeps you out of pace
Your rhythm will be off
that's if you don't submit
And receive the blessings found in Christ
for all that do commit
There's no more cussin, no more drinkin,
no more getting high at all
No more denying who you are in Him
with Jesus you CANNOT fall
Back into the life you had
that voided out your worth
And what was purposed by our God
for you here on this earth
It doesn't matter who you were
it matters who you are
The blood of Christ – His redeeming power
has made you now His star
So take it slow and steady
that be the righteous pace
The favor He bestows on you
is called unchanging *"Grace"*

Be Still

Stop! Don't move I'm talking to you
Right now I need your attention
In stillness there's prevention
That protects you from Satan's wrath
Then places you on My path
But in order to find your way
You must stop be still and pray
Just think how smooth My road is
Much better than your own
And surely that of Satan's
Which you've been on too long
So stop be still and see
That cross the road is Me
Stop be still and find
That needed peace of mind
Stop be still and know
In Me is where you'll grow
Stop be still and chill
Just stop my child be still

Chapter 4

Walk with JESUS

…and the sin power that has ruled your life is now broken!

Walk...signals another Mommy moment as I hear her saying, "Girl, you better pick those feet up and come on!" Oh how, I wish I had. Her exclamatory utterance of course required an immediate action on my part and now I have come to understand, how necessary it was to be intentional when given the command to WALK! What I now know is being intentional about picking your feet up and moving forward, will prevent you from being walked on, walked over and missing many wonderful opportunities in life. That sentence makes me want to cry – but I won't because there is *"HELP"* for the slow walkers like me (smile). However, for those reading this book and have gotten this far and are under the age of 40, don't take too much longer – actually start picking up your feet to get all the goodness that God has planned for you.

Walking in life, at an intentional pace or even at an unintentional pace, has its (pardon the pun) ups and downs but the humbled person, is the great benefactor in either process.

Scenario 1 – It's lunchtime during the hustle and bustle of the workday and Mary is walking to get her lunch. She is walking at an intentional pace and then she stumbles. She then falls after tripping over an imperfection in the sidewalk. She scraps her knee and blood is oozing out but with the quickness of pride and with no assistance, she gets up and brushes herself off and continues her intentional pace back to the office. Now many would consider her a strong women, very confident but no one see's what happens behind the closed door of her office. What happens when the world isn't looking?

Scenario 2 – It's lunchtime during the hustle and bustle of the workday and Margaret doesn't have a care in the world. She strolls along the busy streets as others whisk along and she is not concerned. Her pace in life is her own and then bam, Margaret stumbles and falls over an imperfection in the side walk and just sits there. She looks at the blood oozing down her knee and cry's out, "help me somebody". Many in the world would look at her as weak and lacking self -confidence. Some might even walk past her and say, "Oh, it isn't that bad, she should just get up, wipe it off and keep stepping!"

As mentioned earlier, there is help for both the intentional and unintentional walker. The one that keeps up pace by picking up their feet when given a command as well as the one who lags behind – the helper on both account is Jesus. He knows that hiding from Him will not open the door for help. He also knows that no matter how fast or slow you are walking, if you are walking with Him, you might fall but you certainly won't stay down.

The humbled person wins when they know that falling is a process that leads to growth in Christ and opens the door to God's promises. In 1 Peter 5:6 the Word says that we are to, "Humble ourselves under God's mighty hand, that he may lift you up in due time." How can we be lifted, if we never fall? How can He help us if we hide?

For me, being propped up by Jesus when I finally fell before Him allowed me to see the path I was on could only lead to death. But calling out to Him for help, gave me the ability to step on and step over everything that the enemy had laid before me in my life. All the things that kept me from God's plan and purpose.

My eyes are now fixed on Jesus, my faith is firmly planted in the promises of God and my feet are standing firm on the foundation in

Christ that God planted for each and every one who would believe in His Son.

And I end as I started, today I know that God's mercy is larger than any mistake, disobedience or sin I could possibly make. I now enjoy and encourage others to swing open that narrow gate and walk that path that leads to life, *"for wide is the gate and broad is the road that leads to destruction…"*

I thank God daily for the ones who watched over me and are still watching over me – those ministering spirits that He assigns each of His children. Those angels are at our disposal daily to assist us when we are lost in the storm and looking for the rainbow.

On the day when my hell broke loose I realized that Jesus was always there waiting for me to *Discover Him, Submit to Him, Receive from Him, Walk with Him* and be covered by Him – He's waiting for you too!

Therefore, as you received Christ Jesus the Lord, so walk in him,
Colossians 2:6

What Happens When We Walk With You?

What happens when we walk with *You*
Some might not understand
The obedience that's required
When you're walking in God's plan

What happens when we walk with *You*
And exposure does take place
Revealing all the hidden things
Kept secret behind ones face

What happens when we walk with *You*
Sometimes it hurt so bad
When eyes became wide open
And hearts became so sad

What happens when we walk with *You*
And usual is no more
Replaced with things transformation will bring
To that person who's been restored

What happens when we walk with *You*
They're some who will peel off
But *You*, oh God will add the new ones
That walk the way we walk

What happens when we walk with *You*
On the road that is so narrow
The road that leads to life with *You*
The road that is less traveled

I chose oh God to walk with *You*
The transformed life I live
My minds renewed, my spirits free
And to You my life I give

A Turn of Events

Reflecting on this life to long
the quickening of day and night
The years so swift in how they move
can't tell the dark from light
We teeter totter on circumstances
that cause our light to fade
But brightness we recapture
when no longer we're afraid

Sometimes we ponder regret too long
it really has no place
In what it is that God did plan
while in this time and space
Mistakes and wrong turns have purpose
but should never linger long
They are God's way of building us
to what will make us strong

So release ALL things that have no role
in what God planned for you
An open path to purpose
and what is a brighter view
You'll see God's peace and all He promised
it will guard your heart and mind
And turn the events of a lifetime
into what God always had in mind

Favor

My eyes now see the favor
Of God's promises to me
He blessed me at conception
Now I finally can see
Just what the old folks talked about
When I would listen in
The stories that they shared of God
And where they all had been

"But if not for God's favor", they said,
"Oh Lord where would I be?"
So glad God knew right from the start
Just how to set me free
He sent His Son the only one
Anointed to change things
His Son who bled and died for us
So to Him we now must cling
No longer can we be the ones
The persons we once were
Through favor Christ has given us
The power to conquer

So strut in your new clothes
And be dressed in His grace you see
And wear God's favor on your back
Cause it has made you free
To walk across the stage
After breaking some life rules
But now a graduate with honor
From what was the Hard Knocks School
It's graduation day my friends
walk upright don't be stiff

Salvation is what you received
And Jesus was the gift
You're now a family member
Through Christ you have been saved
Because when they looked He was no more
Inside His earthly grave
He's sitting with the Father
Preparing your special place
The one for you to celebrate
When you meet Him face to face

So find Christ in your actions
Your spirit, heart and mind
And walk in the favor of knowing Him
To help change all mankind

Move Over

What is our purpose in this place
What did God really see
To make Him think that we are worthy
That we could be the key
Instrumental to unlocking
The closed doors of those we know
Well could it be the light we shine
His charge that makes us glow

No more do we hide in life's dark places
His light has made us free
A beam so bright to share with those
Who'll hit the switch and see
That the light that's found in Christ –
The Savior of us all
Was sent by God the Father
Who knew that we would fall
Head first into the things
That make bright lights go out
But when our lights do shine again
We share what His light's about

In Christ you'll find a beam
That seems to never end
A continued replenishing and casting away
Whenever we do sin
So move aside your troubles
The things that life will bring

Walk boldly in the light He shines
Knowing sin has felt His sting
He's perfection, He's our Savior
He's Jesus Christ the Lamb
He's why we now move over
And let Him take command!

When in Life's Valley Season, Count It all Joy

The challenges are many
But You are always there
To cushion the blows for all of us
When we are unaware
Of the trials that lie before us
And the bridges we must cross
The times we are so very confused
The times we feel so lost
The problems mount like snow
That winters bring unknowing
Life's blizzards cover us in many ways
Then faith it seems stops growing
We freeze in unbelief
Not thinking like we should
That this is just a valley season
Once out we'll know we could
That we could have moved much quicker
If only we'd count it joy
And remember in the trying times
It's Jesus we must deploy
And rest on Him the multitude
Of things we don't understand
Cause on the other side of the valley season
Is the mountain on which we'll stand

Don't Miss the Boat

So now that I move with a different stride
That many don't understand
But it's okay cause when they do
They'll want to take my hand
And catch the wave I'm riding
The surf is high this moment
No better time than this my friend
For spiritual atonement
We're in the time of Jesus
To make His second showing
So for the ones who do believe
We can't be easy going
You better pick up your feet
And move with a righteous glide
Cause if you don't you will be left
Like the ones who missed Noah's ride

The Purpose for Which We Exist

The purpose for which we exist
Is not for me and you
The purpose for which we exist
Is to help others make it through
The breath of life we breathe
Given daily from God above
He gives so others will receive
An abundance of Brotherly love
So as we extend a helping hand
And a warm smile showing others
That as we walk to salvation's door
We'll bring another sister and brother

Shelter from the Storm

Come take my hand and walk with me
I'll be your light through me you'll see
That dark is not the place to be
Cause Jesus died to set us free

He opened up the windows
And cleared the storm away
And all the things that keep us where
He didn't want us to stay

So the more you're down please realize
There's goodness in His plan
So come and grab a hold of it
Come on just take my hand

I've seen the dark and what it'll do
to keep you from the light
I know so well just who it is that keeps
the wrong from right
He knows of your potential
Oh yes he does you see
That's why you must rebuke him
And then you'll be set free

My friends the storm has passed
The shelter is in place
The covering is in Jesus
Oh won't you seek His face

I never thought I could do it
Clean up my act so well
The hole I dug was very deep
I too did visit hell

But what I share with you this day
That's if you will conform
Is Jesus Christ the gift of life
The Shelter from the storm!

So… the poetry and prose in this book are messages from
Heaven!
The very words and inspirations God has poured into me, I have poured onto
these pages as I have walked through life's stormy seasons… and I
am now covered under the *"Rainbow"!*

So thankful I am that God chose the medium of poetry for me to
express His message.
So humbled I am that God corrected what use to be "writing wrong
to now writing right!"
I'm forever in awe of my "Daddy" and grateful for His
love, patience and plan for my life.

Thank you Father for my earthly parents, who were
the perfect example of loving without limits.

Thank you Father for those people who have supported my poetry
in one way or another.

You are forever in my heart!

Larry

LBC Family, Roz, Gemma, Nancy, Lou, Shannon, Lawrence, Verna, Stephanie, Angie, Leslie, Darlene, Joyce, Jentzeen, Charles, Joel, Kareem, Emmanuel, Pat, Wille, Lal, Angela, Brian, Diane, Marva, Eboni, Claudette, Dawn, Martea, Molly, Mary, Bill, Brenda, Cornelia, LF Family, Jeremy, Joe, Vincent, Mattie, Thelma, Susan, Everett, Janie, Tamara, John, Yvonne, Alaric, TUBC Family, Patricia, Asbury Family, Tanya, Tanzania

Thank You, Lord

Oh how do I say thank you Lord
for bringing me to this place
I never knew you loved me so
to share with me your grace
You saved me long ago
from the doubt my mother had
And placed me in the loving care
of my adoptive mom and dad

Oh how do I say thank you Lord
I haven't always been good
I wasted so much time in life
not thinking that I could
That I could always depend on you
just as my mother said
The last words that she shared with me
while on her dying bed

She told me I should trust in you
with everything I do
For you would be the only one
to ensure I'd make it through
So with a humble heart of love
I thank you Oh Lord
For being here in all my days
and lifting me with your love

Sincerely,
Paula H. Mathis